WRITERS REPUBLIC

RESTLESS THOUGHTS

THROUGH TIME AND WORDS

KAILASH DARJI

WRITERS REPUBLIC L.L.C.
515 Summit Ave. Unit R1
Union City, NJ 07087, USA

Website: *www.writersrepublic.com*
Hotline: *1-877-656-6838*
Email: *info@writersrepublic.com*

Ordering Information:
Quantity sales. Special discounts are available on quantity purchases by corporations, associations, and others. For details, contact the publisher at the address above.

Library of Congress Control Number:	2022948336
ISBN-13:	979-8-88810-094-3	[Paperback Edition]
	979-8-88810-095-0	[Digital Edition]

Rev. date: 11/01/2022

This is not mere obligation
But my heartfelt dedication
To my kind father and mother
My loving friends and all other
People who have believed
And now I am relieved
That this book is in your hand
I hope you can understand
All the things I wanted to say
I hope you enjoy it, I pray
All the readers around the globe
Can find some solace and hope

1.

Life is like a pitcher
Of wisdom wine
Sip it slowly
You can't just chug it down
Sip it slowly
One day at a time
One moment at a time
And
It will age you with wisdom

2.

Nothing in your body is
At rest
That's why you feel
Restless
You need to move
You can't stay in one place
Like a tree
Because you are a restless soul
A wanderer
A seeker
A traveler
A pedestrian
On the road of life

You need to taste new skies
Drink new oceans
And kiss new stars
You need to fall in love
With mountains
Make friends with rivers and lakes
You want to fly like an autumn leaf
Over the waters of creation

You are restless
You are a star
Made of oldest and newest
Of stardust
Beautiful symphony of the universe
You need to whirl madly
Like a love-drunk Sufi
You need to dance a beautiful violent dance
Like Shiva
You get the urge to jump into the flames of passion
Like a moth
You want to jump off the cliff
Of adventure

You are a restless soul
You desire unfathomable
Love unquenchable
And imagine
Unimaginable
Because even in your biological makeup
You are restless
Nothing in you is still
Not even a fragment of your molecules

That's why
You are restless
Just like we all are
A wandering speck of stardust
A soul of restless eternal flames

3.

The universe is a big river
Wooden floating lanterns
Beautiful
Bright lanterns
Flowing ahead into

They have been flowing
And forevermore
They shall be

We never reach the shores
No one knows if the lanterns do either
But death
Oh sweet glory
Gives us hope

4.

Somebody asked me what is the truth?
What is reality?
What is God?
What is all this?

I said,
I can use all the words I have
Learned
All my life.
Imagine
Until I exhaust to nothing.
Sing every single melody.
Play every single piece of music we have,
And all that is yet to come.
Throw every theory,
Principle,
Axiom,
Number
Or I can stay silent.

Either way,
It's just not enough.
It never is.

5.

Watch the world go backwards on the street.
Smell the dead perfume,
Of the concrete and brick walls.
See the sky cry
Tears of happiness.
I sometimes see
Small toddlers teaching the old,
About life.

I want to ask you.
Have you fallen in love with a smile?
Ever?
Did you ever hear the wind,
Singing to you?
Whispering you stories maybe?
Of all long lost and dead.

I also feel the shivers in the dark.
It just happens.
And have you felt at peace,
In your loneliness?
Do you make your memories compete?
Listening to the music,

Of the universe?

Yes.
I have seen you too.
Only sometimes but,
When you briefly became my comrade,
In unintentionally shared silences,
Moments of longing,
Mutual search of truth,
Of truth!
And that god.

I see the world,
Every day.
And every once in a while,
The world looks me in the eye
And completely,
Utterly embraces me in my vessel
This body of soul.
But ever so instantly,
Immediately,
Suddenly,
Briefly.

I live for these moments,
When I know that
I am not alone.
Would have been a great achievement if I were.
But impossible.

You just can't be alone
With yourself

6.

I look from my window
The crowded roads
Are empty
The people walking
Are no more
The streets are dead
The lights all alone

The travelers are no more
Only the journey remains
I look from my window
And I see
The crowded roads
Are empty

7.

People walk around with
Torn souls
Stitched together with fine
Threads of hope
Destined to suffer and bicker
Fight and chase
With glimpses of joy
Now and then
You people listen to
Me
Your mathematics is wrong

Living off of expectations
Own and other's
They call life many things
Give it many names
Fear of conformity always
Triumphs the passion

You talk to me when you wake up
You talk to me
When you start living
You are still inside cocoon

Come talk to me
When you are a butterfly
And then I will show you
The reason
Behind my everlasting smile
Oh, butterfly
A garden for you

8.

Tonight
I'm in my spot again
Same old bar
Same old strangers

Gulping booze
Drowning themselves in smoke
Rubbing off each other
In rhythm, with music
Just like me
They all are trying to
Forget the emptiness
And the futility of
This life

Because
Tomorrow morning
The world is waiting for
All of us
The world is ready to make us feel puny
Make us feel motivated enough
For its struggles
To continue fighting

To go on

But that's tomorrow
So tonight I'm again
In my spot
I'm in the bar
Drinking booze
And smoking half-burnt cigarettes
Because tomorrow can wait
Till tomorrow

9.

sometimes
life is a remake of
some old unsung song
tears of joy
that has no place in memory
or an echo of the eternal silence
but sometimes
life is a sweet smell of the roses
that are yet to grow
intoxicating taste of the wine
that is yet to be drunk
and
a deep longing of the love
that is yet to come

10.

if you have scars
it means you have stories and
adventures
if your hands are dirty
it means that
you tried
your journey is still a long way
if you feel tired
know that you have to still
walk

if you look over the horizon
every now and then
it means you long for
better tomorrow
if you have a smile
it means you have faith

you are brave
and you have been tested
if you know tears
but if you have
memories of laughter and joy

know that
you have been blessed

11.

death was alone
forever
longing deeply for
something
to feel alive
and he met life
she was beautiful
vibrant with all the colors
of joy and sorrow
love and despair
and so much more

she was perfect
something to fill his void
to complete him
but he couldn't touch her
hold her in his arms
caress her
and tell her about all his
lonely adventures
the pain he felt in
being the death
of others

the moments of happiness he felt
sometimes
and
the dreams he dreamt

because
life would cease to be
the moment he loved her

life too loved his scars
life too
longed to bring him a little bit
of comfort
a lump of starlight
to lighten his dark existence

yet
it seemed impossible

and God said
Love triumphs all

then we were born
children of this eternal love

beautiful life
in the arms of death
maybe that's why

we feel most alive at those moments
that take our breath
away

12.

life is a huge
pitcher
no one knows
who made it
no one knows
when it shall break
we can only
at best
guess

glass half full
or
half empty
maybe
there is no glass at all
but
just the wine

I am a drunk but
what shall I know

13.

when you look at a lake
it feels like
it is ever expanding
and contracting
evermore
never still
turbulent chaos of waves

darker the shadow falling
calmer the water seems
like how eyes are closed
and all seems
alright

14.

I have realized this
since eons ago
before my beginning
in this flesh
and my end
in the soul

that
everything is perfect
all is in perfect harmony
to each other
the good and bad,
chaos and order,
war and peace
and all our futile efforts
trying to do some change
make an impact
in this world

it doesn't matter at all
yet
it does too

everything is completely necessary
the beauty of reality is a paradox
in duality
trying to merge into each other
become one
it is and it isn't

no need to complain
the world was before you
it shall still be here
after you turn to dust
all that humans do
are utterly meaningless
yet
we derive meaning
that is our beauty too

you see
humans can justify anything
war for peace
prison for freedom
hunger for all the killing
and it is completely natural
God is a bastard architect
designing this shithole of the world
leaving us stranded
to find beauty

many break
others thrive

few escape back to God

listen people
everything in the reality is
in right amount
perfect proportions
and
nothing is out of place
or unusual
this life we got
is a terrible privilege
hauntingly beautiful
agonizingly divine
lotus in the mud

15.

Sometimes the world seems too big
and life too short
Other times
the world seems too small
and the life too long
how we go round and round in circles
having adventure of a lifetime

16.

I love the taste of
torn expectations
the flavor of
broken hopes and dreams
it tastes like a cup of coffee
where
neither sugar is enough
nor the coffee
and in the end
it tastes like
too many smiles beaten into heartache
little sweet
but strong and bitter
just my cup
at least it gives me
a decent poem

17.

there I saw a single flower
under the train tracks
still blooming

the train
taking everyone to some place
of their desire
even in its rush
and screech
and journey
couldn't kill the flower
it still grows

I saw that as people's lives
the flower of joy
 passion
love
and all the good things they talk about
and want to relate themselves to
untouched
still intact
forever beautiful

yes, people are like flowers also
like so many other things
and yes
they are the same train
that couldn't kill the flower

but people don't see that
they see themselves as
mere passengers
on a journey to somewhere
me
I see them as a journey too

18.

a monk
falls in love
and he says
how I have been calm
all my life
peace at heart
always
how I longed
never to be unsettled
like a stone thrown in the pond
but
you have been my failure
of that purpose
yet
the most beautiful thing
I have ever felt

a blossom of a flower
called love
in the sunyata of the
enlightenment

19.

everyone asked the Buddha
why did you marry?
the Buddha said
I am Buddha in my head
and my heart
and my soul
and in my
flesh

20.

God is confusion
God is calm too

God is reality
God is paradox too

God is is
God is isn't too

God can be thought
God cannot be too

God is sunyata
the void they say
but God is
everything else too

God is
all and nothing
and beyond them too

I say
beyond words

beyond thought
beyond sunyata
where we shall never reach
is God
and I know
it is both
inside and outside us
but nowhere too

we try to reach God
and we already have
yet
we haven't reached there too

21.

if the sky was burning
would it still be beautiful?
if there was fear of dying?

if the land was flooding
would you be at peace?
knowing you would drown?

can you possibly imagine
death as beautiful?
some would say
yes it is
I know they are lying

I know
they can never
possibly
accept fear as beauty

Or maybe
I am wrong
Yet

You keep saying
Everything is beautiful

22.

I asked God
will everyone
who lived sinfully
wrongly
without realizing their godhood
all their life
before our death
go to hell?

and he laughed
like a thunder
amused at my question
and said
HELL NO!

I love you guys

23.

the other day
someone asked me
what is Zen
I said
keep on painting white
over white
it becomes black
that is
Zen

24.

men make sons
women daughters
kings make kings
like milk butter

but masters
make masters
Like God made us

25.

in the midst of storm
and rain
in the thunder
the flower says,
"this is not what I wanted"
in the spring,
the flower says
again
"that was exactly what I needed
to blossom"

26.

a broken moon
shining down
dying stars
twinkling their last breath
this world,
a big stone turning
turning around an age-old fire
in the vast space of existence

searching to share its load
searching to share life
all alone, too long
waiting to let go

and we
utterly insignificant
dreaming of becoming gods

27.

if unicorns were domestic
and dragons were real
wish phoenix could lay you eggs
I wonder how you'd feel

what would you do if
fishes could fly?
the sea was up above
below was the sky?

why the sky has roses
sunflowers and lilies too
if the sun rose under you
and no breeze ever blew

fireworks of shooting stars
trees came down the zenith
if aurora's mist was everywhere
and cotton clouds beneath

if you could feel the beauty
beyond the realm of real

if you could see from my eyes
I wonder how you'd feel

28.

candy to eye
poison to heart

the world is running out of love
overflowing with sex instead
people die, people suffer
they are busy drawing contest

our principle is better than worse
tragedy is popular news
humanity is merely a word now
and the narcissism is fucking huge

everyone is a philosopher these days
enlightened, awake and mystic
healthy as a damn horse
but delusional inside and sick

self-ostentatious spiritual animals
divine judgmental gods
territorial peace-loving creatures
phony advocating dogs

29.

In the end
Everything dies
Everyone too

The feelings we shed
The smiles we shared
The hearts we broke
And the ones
We mend

Still we go on
Because the show must
They say
That is life

Someone asks me
What is life
I say
Life is wonderful

30.

It's going
further and farther
than it was ever before
and everything seems meaningless

looking from a different
point of view
from very far away
it seems so trivial
so futile even

all that we had held
important
worthwhile
nothing really mattered
really
we didn't matter
really

but
they would say
they will know
they will see that

we existed
we were here
we will be
known

we left our signature
on the fabric of existence

they are content
with their short lives
not me
I will never be happy
I will never be full
I will always be empty

because
I knew
and I still do
I am nothing
I am insignificant
and I fear
I will never
leave this consciousness
and still be awake
aware
conscious
when I meet
God

31.

the world is
a peaceful place
full of beauty, love
and grace
but people have turned it
into a brutal warzone
blinded by greed
and with fear grown
into a dead pond
surrounded by locusts
but I still believe
we all can be lotus
springing from dead mud
with beauty and grace
so still I believe
the world's a beautiful place

32.

They collected all I had
My memories
My books
My paintings
All my tunes
My love

All I had
All I am
And
All I ever will

And were about to
Burn it all
Then
They asked me

Save but one

In that moment
God held my finger
And I smiled
And walked away

33.

Every day is a new experience
But
Why does this newness
Make us old?

34.

A true poet
Can see poetry
In everything
And I mean
EVERYTHING

Not only in rustling of leaves
Not only in shower of rain
In the face of the blue sky
Or
Silence of conscience only

The smell and color of flowers
Or
Every defined encounter
With beauty only

I am not a true poet
So I doubt
Anyone else is too
But
I know in my heart
I am wrong too

35.

People are always saying
That they wish
They were somewhere else
I wish
I never have to wish
I was somewhere else

I want this moment
To forever
Bring me joy

No matter what comes
I wish
I can find joy in it

36.

People want
People to miss them
If needed
Cry for them
Have a warm sunlight
Glow in them too

People want
People to suffer for them
Hurt for them
Yet
At the same time too
People want
People to be elated by them
To remember them
To accept them

People's desire is to be
Desired by people
Special people
Selected by soul
For them

People call it love
Me?
I like to call it
The most beautiful
Paradox

37.

I am just 24
But I feel like a billion years old
There is a bottomless pit
inside my heart
Or
Never reaching height
An infinite sky
Within my soul
Who knows?
'Cause I don't

No matter what
I pour in
It is never full
Or is it full
Already?

Wine
Love
Beautiful and wise
Words from the scriptures
Clouds of smoke
Notes of music

No matter what goes in
They all vanish
Or
Are they all
Already there?

Who knows?
'Cause I don't

And I search
To be full
Or
To empty myself
Who knows?
'Cause I don't

38.

You sit on the bank
Throwing pebbles
Into the ocean
Again and again
Happy looking at the ripples

Yet even if
Surface has waves
The deep is eternally silent
And you have yet to realize
That you are
The ocean

39.

River condescends the pond
For being too stagnant
The pond curses the river
For flowing too much

The sky sees them both
Meeting into the sea
In the end

40.

I see the twinkle in your eyes
That longing for something
Like it never dies
Keep that shine
Burn that fire
It makes your life living
Worthwhile

41.

Look at the beauty
Of a tiny flower
Struggling
Still blooming
Out in the cold and dark
In the snow
Life has adversities
But
It is beautiful too

42.

If I die tomorrow
I'll have no regret
I'll make peace
Believing this is the best I could get

'Cause I've lived my share
And I've also been loved
And in the end
It was all more than enough

43.

Tired words
Sleepless nights
And wandering moon
Spilled on a piece of paper
Blotches of dried whiskey stains
Curtains blowing in the chill of
The silence of the wind
Like white flags of surrender
Waving to the night

Empty streets outside
Nothing awake now
Except for the
Lampposts talking loudly with each other
And brightly
A distant hum of car wheels
Going somewhere
Coming from somewhere
Few undead lights turned on windows
And my neighbor's Doberman barking
At the shadows of the darkness

Half-burnt cigarette butts

The fingers that smell like ashes
In an ashtray of unknown room
An incredibly quiet world waits outside
Drowning in rain
Waiting to be heard

Tides of time come and go
But the night stays awake
For an unknown room
With books on the floor
Unlocked door
Unfinished poems
Unlived memories
And undreamt dreams

44.

God in the heart
And the Devil playing inside the brain
Is a heart full of love
And a head filled with pain
We humans merely flesh and bones
Yet mysterious till the end

45.

Today wages war
In the battlefields of yesterday
To collect the fortunes of tomorrow
And we are the soldiers
Who are born out of time

46.

Some days are just melancholic
Not sad
Not gloomy
Just melancholic

A slight chill in the air
Like it was raining before
But nothing's wet
Misty mountains covered with homes
Like a collection of many stories
And a sun
Hidden somewhere behind the
Cold blanket of sky

Some days are just melancholic
Like it reminds you of yesterday
And the day before
And the day before
And all the days gone by
How this day is passing by too
Slowly
Fading into memory
Bits and pieces

Names and places
Every second
Every moment

Nothing's changed
But nothing is the same
Same old streets
Same old feet
Same old journey
Same old people
But somehow different

Some days
The wind just blows the same
Yet like never before too
Like waving goodbye to
Your beloved again
And the leaves seem greener than usual
Flowers seem happier than
They should be
And the streets
They seem quiet
And empty
Although nothing's changed

Some days are melancholic
Not sad
Not gloomy
Just
Melancholic

47.

Dark circles under the eyes
Callused palms
Tired feet
And aching body

Moving on
Moving on
We keep fighting
One day at a time
Ever trudging forward
Slowly but surely
Going on

Time goes on
Seconds pass
Minutes and days
Weeks and months
Years then pass by
But we get nowhere
We began nowhere

Just a dream
Just an illusion

Of getting somewhere
Being nowhere
Becoming somebody
Fighting nobody

But life goes on
And we go along
Unstoppable
Unreachable
For a long-lost dream
A mirage
A shadow in the dark

But feet are not meant to be
Stopped
Eyes can't stop dreaming
And hands get burnt
Every time
They reach for the stars

Oh, Icarus
But
How we learn
To never learn

48.

A poem is a song
It is a movie
A piece of craftsmanship
A sculpture

It is a memory
And also a vision
Hard reason
And warm feeling too

A poem is nostalgia
Awe
Beauty
Agony
And ecstasy too

A poem is a story
On a sheet of paper
It is a journey
And destination too

A poem is a dream
A longing

A call
A scream
An escape
And a refuge

A poem is a collection of mere words
Yet so much more
Transcending those same words
A poem is a soul
A window
A door
And a house

A poem is an idea
A possibility
It can be anything
As long as it is read
Like life
Anything to make of
As long as it's lived

49.

Graffiti walls
Empty railway tracks
Half-built skyscrapers
And blank sky

Approaching twilight
The day waving goodbye
The calm before the storm
The rush hour to get home

Lonely trees in sad landscapes
Ancient lights and electric poles
With wires barely holding up
A sign of departure
For today
For now

Done for the day
Done for today
An end of one short adventure
Merely 24 hours long
Stretched along eternity
Tired

And exhausted

The sun slowly hiding behind the hills
Somewhere far away
Dead leaves kissing him goodbye
Just to see him
Another day

Summer breeze blowing
Calm and cold
Whispering an invitation of night
Like those graffiti on the walls
On the way home

Unclear messages
For unknown strangers
Going somewhere

The graffiti starts to fade
Houses grow smaller
Streets get narrower
But electric wires still hold on
To those ancient poles
And train tracks
They keep running
All night long

Because
The journey must go on

50.

People passing by
Strangers on their way
Like everyone else
Like every day
A new story is woven with
Every new step
Something lies waiting
For everybody

People on streets
People at work
People on holiday
People
Everywhere

Each footstep lands on the ground
With a silent touch of faith
In tomorrow
In today
In yesterday

Walking ahead
What a simple act of belief

Courage
And hope

51.

We are not cowards
Yes
We fear death
But when it knocks on our door
We shall dance with it
Just before we go
Once
Maybe just once
We shall show death
What the music of life is
We'll make sure
Death sings our tune
Before it takes us away

We are not cowards
Having fear is not cowardice
Fighting through life
Is not the only courage
Accepting death is too
And yes
We shall make death smile
Once
Maybe just once

Before we go
We shall make him proud
Of the life we lived
The life he is taking

52.

Death dissolves all
A universal solvent
An inescapable fate
A goodbye in the end

There's no broken heart
There's no grieving soul
Nothing in this world
That death cannot mend

No mountain it cannot melt
No ocean it cannot drink
No sky it cannot shrink
Nor a second it cannot spend

But don't be afraid
He's just a lonely man
Quietly extending his hand
Like an eternal silent friend

53.

"Who never gets tired of giving?"

"Mother."

"No. That's God."

"That's the same."

54.

A balloon of fire floats high in the sky
A cold silver rock shines quietly at night
A thousand splendid fireflies in eternal flight
Keep burning on to give off the light

In the home of a mad swirling stardust
Forlorn from the rest and completely lost
Like a tiny speck of sand blazingly burst
Blowing in the wind with a divine gust

Little creatures with hope there live
In something mystical and magical believe
Hoping at last salvation they'll receive
For all the years they shed and toils they give

Circle keeps spinning, life goes on
In a mere mortal world meant to turn
Learning to fly, they walk, stumble, and run
Longing for meaning, with deep imagination they burn

In an ever-growing void so vast
Wondering about the shadows they cast

Caught in the stream of future, present, and past
An endless whisper, perhaps mere echoes at last

55.

I close my eyes and
Chase will-o'-the-wisps
I chase them towards the
Dreams unknown
Lands unknown
Faces unknown

I do it because
Outside the world burns
War ravages
Peace kneels down and asks
For mercy
Hypocrisy puts on a fake face
Of compassion
Of love
And
Humanity
It all becomes too much
To bear

Words no longer mean anything
Actions almost always
Are just a front

The trees cry
The oceans plead
Even the air they breathe
Begs them for help
But they cannot hear
Their ears are covered with earphones
And
Latest trends of music
Their eyes are glued to the screens
Like moth gazing into the fire
It all becomes too much
To see

Escaping is sometimes the only
Option
I close my eyes and chase
Will-o'-the-wisps
Because the way I see it
Is better than chasing shadows
Better than chasing your
Own tails
Maybe that's why they say
The world goes round and round
Maybe the world keeps
Chasing its own tail

They want to trust
But cannot stop lying
They want to build
But cannot stop killing

Progress they say
Development they call it
Upgrading the life as they
Go on
Newer version
Better models
They say
Yet
Same old ways
Chasing tails

So it all becomes too much
To bear
Too much to see
For me, so I just close my door
Close my eyes
And chase will-o'-the-wisps
Chase them towards the
Dreams unknown
Lands unknown
Faces unknown

56.

From kindness we are nurtured, from kindness we grow
Only through selfless love, our true colors we show

A tough place to live, this world they say
Tough is its name, even tougher is its way
Lest we forget, we have souls like stars
That bright with compassion, in darkest hours glow

A hard-fought battle with struggles and pain
Scorched in deep sun, drenched in cold rain
We make sacrifices for the dreams we dream
An act of valor and faith, even the gods know

Chasing a lost shadow of reflection of time
A free-spirited ember that nothing can bind
Setting ablaze everything, we move hand in hand
Through highest of the high, and lowest of the low

We keep wiping tears and sweat off each other's brow
Each other is all we got, only through kindness we grow

Only through selfless love, our true colors we show
If you still doubt me, try being human and you'll know

57.

If you give up now, if you surrender
You will stay soft, you will grow tender

Hardships and struggles are just life's way
Stand, dust yourself up, it's just another day

So many more battles await further ahead
So never give up, not until you're dead

Do not expect anything, for your life to be
For it is way beyond what you feel, know, or see

If this life be a challenge, like people say it is
Then never bow down, never fall on your knees

Some battles are lost, some battles are won
But what matters most are the things that you learn

You'll get cracks on your armor, scars on your blade
Just remember to breathe and never be afraid

When life brings you down and makes you feel like cheated

Remember you are a warrior who can never be defeated

58.

Overlooking the ocean
Lives an old park bench
Trees all around
Green carpet of grass
A playground for dogs
Relaxing spot for people
All hide behind him
And
Before him is
Only
A fence
And behind it is
The Ocean fence couldn't
Hide from him

The old park bench just waits
Silently
Quietly
For people to sit on him
Dogs to pee on him
Teenagers to carve
Their initials
Vandals to write something

Provocative
Or suggestive
Or amusing
Or something else

He listens all the time
Not only the murmur of ocean
But also the people
Who sit on him
Their conversations
Their stories
The budding romance of young kids
Their rebellion too
Tragedy and hardships
Happiness and laughters
Smiles
And
Tears too
He listens to everything
Even the dogs barking
Growling
Howling
Sometimes whining
But
Never disturbing them
Never interrupting them
Silently
Quietly

He is slowly aging
Day by day
Weeks, months,
Years
He loves the sea though
Loves the people
Loves the dogs
The young kids
And the ruffians too

Slowly he is breaking
Slowly
He is wasting away
One of his legs
Is broken
He is getting molds
In corners and other places
And starting to look ragged
Nowadays
He rarely gets visitors
People don't sit on him much
He hasn't got any new carved
Initials of young lovebirds
In a long time
The rowdy bunches too don't seem to
Get excited
To spray or paint on him
Anymore
Even the dogs
Don't pee on him

Nowadays

But he still listens to
People talking
People getting older
A little wiser
Young hearts getting broken
Young hearts getting mended
Talks of lost dogs
New dogs
Good dogs
Bad dogs
Big dogs
Small dogs
The young rebels growing up
New ones coming
Some changing ways
Some staying same
He still listens
Or tries to anyway
His hearing is not as good
As it used to
Be
Maybe he is hearing things
Maybe it's the grasses
Whispering in disarray
Or
It's just old age

But inside he smiles
He looks over the ocean
And the fence
The fence smiles at him
And he smiles back
Because he knows
It's a wonderful day
In the park
Today

59.

There was once
A full moon
He was looking
Around
The world

He was looking down on valleys
And mountains
And snowcaps
The forests
Rivers
Ponds and
Streets

Houses
People
Cities and countries
Floating islands
On earth

Then he saw
The Ocean

And the Ocean saw him

She could give him nothing
only mirror of
His image
Constant
Ripples of waves
Some deepest darkest secret
Within her depth
Many untold stories
Unborn yet
Within her heart
A fearful calm silence
Within her soul

How
He saw her waves
Like the ebb and flow
Of a longing quiver
Like a heart
Beating in love
Beating for him

And he forever
Fell in love
Never really falling down though
Hanging from the sky's ceiling
And she couldn't really rise either
Try as she might
Laid like a carpet

Kailash Darji

On the earth's floor

There was once a moon
He was a
Fool moon

60.

I was walking down the store
To get me some milk
And I saw
A running man in shorts
Making me wonder
Why do you run?
Is something chasing you?
Or
Are you
Chasing something?
You are not a hypocrite
Are you?

Do you run because
You had too much to
Eat?
Or you have too much
Time at hand?
You are not the same man who
Talks of being vegan
Are you?
Talking of animal cruelty
While the world goes hungry

Surely you can't be the
Man who saves dogs
From the pound
But cannot adopt a child
I must be mistaken
I am sorry
You wouldn't rather feed that homeless war veteran
Down by the road,
Would you?
Nah,
You are a busy man
You wouldn't

But tell me again
Man running in shorts
Early morning
In the scorching noon
And in the chilling evening
Too
Surely you are not
A fake
A pompous philosopher of humanity
Are you?
You would rather kiss the trees
Than
Kiss these beautiful people scarred by life,
Would you?
You would
Opt to train your cats

Than train your children,
Or would you?

You would rather exchange your lover
Than
Mend their broken soul
I am sorry
Am I being too honest?
Or too cruel?
I must be mistaken
You cannot possibly be the same
Man
I am thinking of

Well
I gotta go
And get my milk
You keep running
Maybe you'll change the world someday
Maybe we'll
See each other again

61.

Oh, moon!
My love
What mirage are you?
How I long you
The chrysanthemum falls slowly
Gently
With a pink blush
Palm trees stand tall
Yet shy
The sky turns blue
Giggling so softly
And a little purple too
With a sliver of doubt

The horizon keeps calling
The mist keeps falling
And yet you hide behind the veil
Of the reflection of the
Deep beloved ocean

The chrysanthemums bloom again
And the moon peeps back again
From behind the veil

Clouds start to flutter
Shine in the moonlight
Like a lover's image
In the sleeping twilight
Welcoming the dreams
Silently
Quietly
Falling asleep

Oh, moon!
My love
What mirage are you?

62.

Resiliently smiling
Like warm sunshine
Against the dark skies of the world
Of the society

You can see the fight
Twinkling like a blazing star
In her ocean-blue eyes
She walks unafraid
Yet gracefully like a cat
Unhazed
Unfazed
Unabashed

Her fingers are slender and beautiful
Thunderbolts of experience
And struggles

She has fought her battles
The dents in her armor
Are proof
Ask her about some scars
She is a warrior

She never bows down
Never surrenders

A living proof of
Creator curating too

You know
You have tried to chain her
With your rules
And your system
Your prejudices
Yet she rises
Higher and higher
Your chains merely snowflakes
In her wake

A living goddess
Strong and soft
Violent yet coy
Braver than you know
But still kind
A heart of gold
And a mind so bold
Ah!
The greatest wonder!

That's why she is called beautiful

63.

I have no regrets
My race is run
For what it's worth
It was fun

The praises I got
And all the scorn
They were all lessons
I had to learn

Like an eagle to fly
Like a candle to burn
My purpose is complete
My metaphor is done

I fought with my God
And I battled my Demon
I don't fear death
I'm just happy I was born

64.

Dark is my color
Dark is my heart
Dark is the world's play
Darker still my part

Dark my shadow illusion
I, a child of dark art
Dark in the end
Always darker from the start

Dark is life's chariot
From darkness never apart
I came from darkness
And from darkness I'll depart

65.

The lines on his face
They read like prose
His smile looks
Like a secret untold story
The gray in his hair
Speak of legends unknown
And his calloused hand
Feels like battered armor
From countless battles
And smells like myth too

He is just a man
And he looks
Like an aged mountain
Tall and standing high
Yet still mysterious
Just like a crossword

66.

A solace for trembling hearts
A refuge for runaways
A lump of candlelight for those who fear the dark
Love is magic
For those who've stopped believing

It's a prayer
A miracle for the seekers
And a companion for those who walk alone

Love is an escape
A safe haven
A catching of the breath when the world's just too much
Something
That makes you feel alive

A jump in your heartbeat
A gleam in your soul
And a smile on your face
Love is sunshine
To your dull and gray day

Love is the solution

A reason for joy
An eternal salvation
And sometimes
A terrible privilege

67.

I hear the trains screeching
To a halt
They stop
They go
They come
And they wait

Never still
Ever running

Sometimes they carry passengers
Sometimes passengers carry them
Sometimes people get to their destinations
Other times
Only trains do

But it goes on
Back and forth
On and on
Through the morning
Through the night
Never sleeping

Never tired

I hear the whistles blow
I hear the announcements loud and clear
Clear through the afternoon traffic
Clearer in the cold winter night

How people never sleep
How they don't let the trains sleep too
An eternal travel
A lifelong journey
Going somewhere
Leaving somewhere
How repetitive
How boring
How natural
How necessary

As long as you wait for me
Oh, trains!
Be a little quieter
Be a little subtle
It's a cold winter night
The day was very tiresome
And I have to go to sleep
For I have to see you again
Early in the morning

68.

There's something to this air
Something else to this light
How the candles burn softly
Yet a little deeper
The winter breeze kisses my windows
Smearing it with misty stains of
Lipsticks
And the curtains shy
Twirl away
With a blush of vermillion
A dab of dainty yellow
How the shadows keep dancing
With every flicker of the flame
Like a story in motion
A song playing
Or a poem happening

This night keeps itself awake
Droopy eyed
Slowly slipping into dreams
With every second the wick burns quietly
Their faint audible crackling whispers
Echoing in the still darkness

Of my room

But I stay vigilant
Awake and waiting
For the candles to go to sleep
For the night to go to sleep

69.

She knew I belonged to her
From the first time
She saw me
And I knew
She belonged to me

She loved me
And I loved her
More than anything
She was my everything
She let me in her life
She let me be family
She took me inside
Her heart

Evening walks in the park
Watching movies together
Playing silly games like Frisbee
It was all so beautiful
So full of life
Only with her

She always told me how much she loved me

But I could never tell her back
I could only
Bark
And wag my tail
Maybe lick her face
Her hand sometimes
I wish in those moments
That I could speak
So I could tell her
How much special she was
To me

When I started smelling her different
I wanted to tell her
I knew she was going to be sick
But she wasn't aware
I knew
I could only bark
And surely enough
She got weaker
And weaker

Her beautiful eyes turned dim
She couldn't walk no more
We couldn't watch movies no more
But I still loved her
She was still my human
I was still her best friend

And she left one day

Even after my countless vigilant nights
By her bedside
After I stayed awake many a nights
Fending off the demon that was
Coming to take her
Keeping an eye on that door
Protecting her
Like I was always told to
Like I was meant to
Like I always loved to

She used to tell me
Everything
She used to tell me I know
Everything
I certainly didn't know she was going to leave me
I certainly didn't know
I couldn't protect her
For all the love she gave me
For all the life she gave me
And her friendship

If there's another life
I wish to be a dog again
And I wish she would love me again
But what do I know
I am just a dog
I can't even talk
I just bark and
Wag my tail

70.

He was weak
My father in his last days
Bedridden and terminal
In pain and very uncomfortable
Getting old is not easy he said
But
Someone was always there to look
After him
Stay close to him

Once I was with him
His six-year-old daughter
And he asked for water
I went to get it
In the kitchen
And when I came back
He had stopped breathing

She had been a fighter all her
Life
She was a pro boxer actually
But she had cancer
One opponent she couldn't knock out

One fight she couldn't win
But she never gave up
Never gave in

Her head was shaved
Her eyes lost their gleam
But she still smiled
Her shoulders hung loose
Her fingers grew brittle
But she still was a fighter
Her spirit was waning
But she never showed that

And when her nurse left her side
To check on other patients
She had already tapped out
She had left the ring
By the time the nurse came back

He was only seven
But boy he was strong
He wanted to be Spiderman
He wanted to play outside
Run with other kids
But he had leukemia
Oh, what a shame!
How utterly unfortunate!

Before he learned how to live

He had to learn how to die
In an age he was meant to grow
And read
And run
And dance
And sing
He was in crutches
He was in agony

His mother died inside every time she
Saw him
It was unbearable to her
How can it not be?

And with droopy eyes
Yawning, and in bed
He asked her to call his father
When they came back
He was no more

It is very tragic
And perhaps frightening
When you have to face death
Alone
Making people close to you wish
They could face death with you
Hold your hand
And make it easy for you
But they know they can't

And that kills them inside

God seems cruel sometimes
It's not his fault
It's nobody's
It is what it is
Death is necessary
Death is also very unfair many times

Because life is a beautiful thing
We cherish it
But death
Death is inevitable
It hurts
Tremendously
And is hard to accept
But we simply can't escape it

71.

Broken fan standing
In a corner
Head turned away
An old guitar standing on the bathroom door
Attached
In my room
The lights are on in the bathroom
The heater is on too
'Cause that is the only light
In my room
That works

I am marveling at the engineering
Of the architect

A slowly dying cigarette
Quietly creeping up to
Kiss the fingers
And scorch them for waiting
Too long

A canvas half filled
Half colored

Half empty
Half full
Hangs in a corner another
Like a frame of life

It smells in here!
Something old and forgotten
Something left alone for far too
Long
Like an envelope
Sent to an abandoned,
Still unopened
In the mailbox,
Lost house

I hear whispers of the dead
Echoes of memories in my room
A calling out perhaps
The walls cracking
Windows broken
The curtain stained with withered expectations
They all seem very
Surreal

My suitcase lies on the floor
Mocking me with a smirk
Laughing at me
For it knows
We will be walking out of here
Soon

Just like many other rooms before
Just like many other stories
Before

72.

What a world we live in
What people we live with
All glass people
You just rub them the wrong way
And
They crack

73.

Some people are like telescopes,
They aim big.
And others are like microscopes,
They enjoy little things in life.

And then
There are people
Like kaleidoscopes

74.

The whisper of lightning
The quiet murmur of night
The sky humming a song;
A song blowing in the wind
The trees dancing
To the tune of the cold air
Coming from the sea
Playing touch-and-run
With the waves

The rowdy laughter of thunder
The teasing drizzle of rain
The leaves
And the flowers
And everything getting wet
With every falling raindrop
Blushingly wet like a love
Yet untainted by the world
Yet unleft by innocence

The sands from the shores
Are slowly getting pulled into the ocean
One grain at a time

One wave at a time

I see somebody walking
Walking barefoot on the shores
Wet in rain
I see that the waves sneak up close enough
To steal the footprints away
One grain of impression at a time
One forgotten memory
At a time

My window wouldn't close
The curtains are all wet
Now
That somebody is still walking
Still getting drenched in the rain
Still going further and further away
Steadily
Slowly

I look at the moon
She also doesn't know
Who that somebody was
She is the only thing
Yet not wet
In the sky
While the stars are twinkling
And
Shivering in cold

I look at that somebody
Still going
Now just a dark blob
In the darkness of night
Way further up ahead
Like a shadow
Moving through the night

My wife calls me back to sleep
I tell her
Somebody's out in the rain at this hour
This hour of exactly 2:39 a.m.
Lazily she gets up
Comes to the window
And looks outside

"Maybe some weirdo,
Come back to bed,"
She says
I shrug to myself
I give a long yawn
And go back to bed

Outside
The thunder is laughing
It is still raining
And I'm pretty sure
That somebody is still going
Don't know where

But
Definitely still going

75.

You are you,
And I am me.
Isn't it amazing?
Just to be.
To walk the Earth
Touch, feel, and see
And live our own life
Completely free

76.

She's a hard work for sure
When needed, she can be tough
But she's got a soft heart hidden
Trust me I know, all she needs is love

She's not some broken soul to rescue
She's not your fairy-tale princess
She's a woman complete in herself
Not some poor damsel in distress

She's full of hopes and aspirations
She's also made of losses and sorrows
A mind of her own in her own ways
Building her own better tomorrows

She's much more than the way she looks
And so much more than the way you see
With her wings wide open blocking the sun
She walks down the world proud and free

She is a woman who carries herself
With beauty, elegance, and such grace
But beware of masks she puts on for society

She's not just some another pretty face

A woman she is strong and kind
A woman so loving, brave, and bold
Unfazed, unhazed, and unafraid to be
The way she is in front of the world

77.

She was a book but she wasn't a reader
She just wanted somebody who would read her

Full of stories and puzzles and poem
She was like a house, waiting to be a home

The chapters that made her, they were strange
They longed for new words, they longed for change

Deep secrets there were written on the pages
Left unread and hidden from people since ages

She asked for nothing but patience sometimes
For people to try and read between her lines

78.

The waves of time come and go
Where the anchors drop, only waves know

We mere humans on a voyage to land
At the mercy of the water we don't understand

But brave enough and surely stupid we are
With an eye on the horizon that's never too far

Going on with the sails set high
Dreaming with stars and learning to fly

And surely there must be a land as told
Or what possibly could so much water hold?

For we can't forever be floating about
With the waves of ignorance and of doubt

Like all mountains crumble into the sand
Like all stories of ocean long for the land

Just so we are also going places

Where we belong with our unmasked faces

City of thousand magnificent suns
Where endlessly the cornfield runs

Or a land of a million colorful lights
Covered with clusters of supernovae at nights

Or someplace secret where you can just be
To just sit back at the world and see

Nonetheless we are on a boat sailing
Where is the shore, there's no telling

But faith we have in waters we are
And travel we must and go too far

79.

Who do you write for?
For yourself or for others?
If you can't enjoy the writing itself
Why do you bother?

I see you write to impress
So your words are all fake
I can't see the beauty of writing
A poetry for just its sake

Your words are all hollow
Just like a sand castle
With a mere touch of waves of time
It will all crumble and fall

I see you need an audience
I see you need a theater
If only you could forget all these
What you say would be so much better

But you too are wise you say
You say you are smart

Kailash Darji

I know you will say you'll do
Whatever comes to your heart

I'm sorry I can't trust your words
Trust me I tried believing you
But every time I read your words
They just all feel so untrue

I see the kind of life you lead
And how you go about your ways
All you crave for is attention
You write 'cause you just want to be praised

80.

Stranded on an empty roadside
Of an unknown town
Night is upon me
Nothing around
Nobody in sight
Except some screeching tires
Somewhere far away
Some echoing lights
Blinking on the lonesome streetlights
Waiting for someone to pass them by
Waiting for something to walk by

I light a cigarette
And another one
And another one
Until my lips turn bitter
And my fingers smell like burnt ashes
Until the air starts to smell
Like smoke
Until the streetlights ask me to stop
I want to go on
But I don't

I move from where I was leaning
A small fence bar
Broken and tattered
Left all alone
All its compatriots dead and fallen
Already on the ground
The wires that held them
Tired and lifeless

I need to walk
But to where
I ask myself where should I go?
If I'm really lost,
Does it matter which way I go?
If it doesn't matter which way I go,
Am I really lost?

81.

No lingering memories
Of yesterday
No tempting aspirations
Of tomorrow
I am a man of today
Walking between the ebb and flow
Of times long gone
And the days unborn yet

Today is all I have
Today is all I ever had
Maybe that's why I suffer so much
For I do not miss my yesterdays
And I cannot remember
My tomorrows

82.

Never tiring, never faltering
These feet are made to walk
While these ears may hear words of doubt
And lies this heart may trust
These feet go on walking
To the place where we belong
Where we deserve

Sometimes these eyes
They don't see very clear
And this old wretched soul
Feels tired and wants to give up
These can't reach out
And hold on to the dreams
And these faces too wrinkle
And fall
But these feet
They keep on walking ahead
Never stopping
Never crying

The skin withers slowly
The smiles grow weak too

The tears, they all dry up inside
And the hairs turn gray and bald
Even in the darkest of hours
Even in the loneliest of times
When words are lost
And ears go deaf
When smiles are abandoned
And cries grow too weak
These feet keep on walking still
'Cause they know
They always know
The place where we need to be
The place we call home

83.

Dreams are the windows to the soul
Or so I have been told
Are they some calling from the universe?
Or a shout-out to the world?

I don't know where they come from
I don't know where they go
Do they come from inside me?
Or from somewhere outside I don't know

They make me see the things
I would miss and normally ignore
Do they really have some meaning?
Is there really something they show?

They hide and whisper, slowly and softly
From someplace strange and unknown
I wonder where they lie inside me
I wonder where they grow

Where do dreams sprout their wings?
I wonder through what land they flow
What city of winds do they reside on?

Through what mystic valley they blow?

But they come and go as they please
At the skies of deep sleep they glow
They come and envelop me quietly every night
They tread ever so soft and slow

84.

There's a voice inside you
That screams for more
Longs for more
Seeks the impossible
Reaches for the unattainable
Looks for the invisible
Loves the imperfections

There's a longing inside you
That wants to find something worthwhile
Something worth dying for
Something worth
Living for
And growing old serenely

The voice keeps knocking inside that door of yours
All the time
Opens the windows of your soul
And the roads of your heart
It keeps pounding on that self-made cage
To be set free
It doesn't let you sleep
It doesn't let you rest

Just so you can find peace within yourself

It goes on and on
Like it's meant to be there forever
But it doesn't
It doesn't last forever
At least not in most people

As time goes on
And people "grow up"
The world keeps weighing heavy on the shoulders
The ground keeps burning under the feet
But you keep dragging on
And slowly
But steadily
Maybe stealthily
The voices grow weaker day by day
As the clock hand ticks ahead
One second at a time
One moment at a time
Until it goes silent
Completely and utterly quiet

And people think they have reached
They think they have found peace
But they don't realize
Most people don't understand
It's the voice of their soul
Their passion growing mute
It's the silence of the echoes of their passion buried

Under the rubbles of the world's affairs
It's the sound of their soul
Dying
It's the sound
Of life
Dead

85.

Humans
Such fragile yet strong creatures
Flickering flame of burning
Dazzling light
A twinkling star
Amidst the flux of what was
And what could possibly be

A moment of being
Just passing through the
Memories of echoes long dead
And the calling of the times unborn yet
Sailing through the ocean of
Nostalgia of past from yesterday
And the imagination of future from
Tomorrow

Carrying the weight of existence on their shoulders
Walking with the burning embers of ever following
Death under their feet
Yet their head too strong
To walk the path that lies
Ahead

And their heart too good
To suffer all the pain

Ever reaching out their hands
To touch the untouchable
Human beings
Soaring through the skies of creation
Longing for beyond
A traveler through time and space

86.

You may lie, you probably will cheat
But I speak the truth, this is it
Don't hurt my pride, don't you ever dare!
'Cause I won't show, I'll just stop to care

When in anger, yes, the truth you speak
And I know for once what you seek
You lend a hand and act like my friend
But all in all I know you just pretend

Your words are all hollow, your actions too steep
The evil in your heart that lies too deep
I see its glances in the way you play cool
And the way you try to treat me like a fool

Yes I am gullible, yes I am slow
If that is all it takes for you to show
What you really are made of, what you think
That sweet poison you smile and give me to drink

Oh, what magnificent and magnanimous you act
Ignorant of all the virtues you lack
You tell me to fly, such words of vain

Yet offer me the wings made of chain

But now I see the mask on your face
I've learned my lesson and now I know best
All I have to do is stay quiet and see
The act you put on, what you keep pretending to be

87.

Nobody knows the hurt you've been through
But listen to my words because they are true
Nothing lasts forever, not even your pain
Not even those bunch of crowds who call you insane

You may not belong anywhere, you may be an outcast
You may feel lost and that the world's moving too fast
You may not want to wake up and face the day
But you're stronger than your fears, ignore what others say

They don't know you, they haven't lived your life
The war you carry inside your soul and your head full of strife
Patience is a virtue, good things do come slow
You will find the place where you belong, time will surely show

You will find your tribe, you will find your home
You will find someone who'll understand and call you their own
You may walk this land alone for now

But have faith in yourself beyond all doubt

Slowly but steadily, you are going where you should be
On an invisible road to the place only your soul can see
So get up and keep on fighting, one day at a time
Because you're meant to kiss the moon and grasp the stars
Soaring through the sky

88.

Surrender to the calm, surrender to the quiet
Sleep my child, go gently into the night
Give yourself to sleep, slowly let go
Slowly let dreams come and let them show

A world beyond this one, some faraway land
Do not be afraid, just let them take your hand
Close your eyes and welcome the sleep
Fall ever so softly in that warm silence deep

Do not worry my child, for you are just resting
You will wake up again just like a sun setting
Let your eyes go heavy as dreams are calling
Like a soft feather in the dark silently falling

Do not be afraid my child, it is not the end
Just as much as the light, dark too is your friend
Mother is here sleeping by your side
Sleep my child, go gently into the night

89.

No emperor ruled forever
No kingdom won the race
Against the time
And stood tall through eternity
No mountain held its head high
In pride forever
And never bowed down
Never was there a warrior
Who never ever lost
Nor there was ever a saint
Who never ever sinned

There never bloomed a flower
That stayed forever young
There never lived a man too
Who never died
No door has been ever there
That stayed forever closed
Or a window that was
Open always
Or a road that has never been
Walked
Or a pair of eyes

That have never cried
Or a pair of lips
That never parted and smiled

For what was will never forever be
Things pass
Such is the nature of all things
Perhaps the only permanent thing
Is change
It keeps blowing like the seasons
Unabashed
Unpredictable
Inevitable
And moves things away
Takes things away
Brings things away
To what they weren't
To what they could be
Or what they should be

Such is the nature of change
Of impermanence
To create things that didn't exist
A moment ago
Yesterday
Or from the past
And slowly push them into the
Possibilities of the future
To the realm of tomorrow

But what is past?
What is the future?
Change is irrelevant to these
Change is unaware
Such is the nature of things
In the end perhaps
Change is just a vagabond wind
Merely blowing through existence

90.

I ran from this, I hid from that
I couldn't be anything so I became art
I spilled on the pages as words into poem
Finally I found a semblance of a home

I threw my soul with every brush stroke
Painted myself on the canvas until I broke
I bled my agony through every string
I played my heart's tune and all the suffering

I chased my longings, I ran after dreams
Until I calmed down my soul's screams
I made my heart and my head friend
To keep me company until the very end

91.

Barely surviving, hanging by a thin rope
Swimming in despair devoid of any hope
The world keeps on coming crashing down
You can't feel anything and you slowly drown

You feel like it's the finish line, you let go
You just want to give up 'cause you don't know
It all becomes too much to bear and just enough
The road seems to never end, ever so rough

You feel like there's no one that can save you
Everything seems so mundane, nothing exciting and new
The routine kills you, the day burns your skin
The night gives you chills like you can never win

That voice inside you tells you to just run away
But it's always darkest before the brightest day
Let time heal you my friend, trust me on this
Have faith in yourself, you will find peace

You will heal, you will shine, you will be all right
Just hold on to yourself and get through this night

It feels like the end but it's just the beginning
But if you just don't give up, you will find meaning

All the pain and suffering, they will light your way
You can move ahead only if you may
Stop stopping yourself from growing and running
Just believe in yourself, time is slowly turning

There is surely a light at the end of the road
Keep on walking and carry life's heavy load
Someday you will look back and be glad you stayed
You will be proud of the story you've made

You will find everything you've ever hoped for
You just have to see it through until it's all over
Just keep on fighting even if you're alone
Just bear the pain a little longer and it will all be over
and done

92.

The day sets with the sun
Slowly the night takes its shape
Perhaps that is the only way
The blazing tired sun can escape

The moon takes its place
Quietly rising in the night sky
Calling all its twinkling stars
Bidding the burning sun goodbye

The sun takes a break from glowing
And all the stars take their turn
Moon climbs silently up the hill
With a soft silvery shine to burn

The vigilant owls start to hoot
The north wind brings its chills
The twilight welcomes the darkness
With all its hidden secret thrills

The moon smiles daintily high
With the shine borrowed from the sun

This hide-and-seek of sun and moon
Such an eternal cosmic fun

The night envelops everything around
Dispersing the dreams of tomorrow
The moon and stars tell you to sleep
As the darkness of night steadily grows

You look at the moon glow and shine
Like a mirror to the sun's warm light
It tells you that the sun is still there
Just hidden out of your sight

So listen to the leaves rustling
And the north wind whispering quiet
To welcome the sunrise next morning
The moon bids you sweet goodnight

93.

She doesn't want to leave me
Oh my night! she keeps me awake
To a land of such wonderful dreams
Full of adventures we escape

Together we go on a journey
Across the deep stars and space
To find familiar strange lands
On a wild, wild goose chase

Of what fun we have together
My night and me in our sleep
'Cause she is the only one who knows
All the secrets that I keep

She knows all of my longings
She knows all of my muses
She knows all my parlor tricks
And all my faulty ruses

She is my beautiful mistress
I hide her secretly from the world

We live in dreams what never happened
And we relive the memories old

We fly through the valleys and plains
We swim across the whole universes
We watch the movies never made
And we read such unwritten verses

We feel scared, we laugh and cry
We live lives that could never be
Oh, my dark love! My beautiful night
The things we together see

So I love to close my eyes
And let her embrace me so tight
'Cause the best adventures I ever have
I only have with my love, my night

94.

When it begins, nature always starts with the green
That's the way the spring has always been
The leaves of grass and the leaves of tree
Spring seems so new with the skies ever so clean

Flowers start to blossom, earth wakes up again
All the beasts and fowls start dancing across the plain
The days grow softer, the nights grow lovely
All turns lively and novel with plenty of rain

Melting away the winter blue, oh, such sweet fragrance!
The whole world turns into a garden for the butterflies
to dance
The air carries the breeze of joyful enthusiasm
Nature takes her turn this time to show her divine
elegance

Spring always comes with the hope of a mending,
A happier tomorrow that forgets yesterday's lamenting
Baptizing the souls of mortals, making them believe
In the magnificence of the nature's beauty never ending

95.

You walk, you little humans
Happy with your lives
With your scheduled routines
All the time
On and Off of your routine
Your desires and dreams held on a
Platter
Held on a pause
You pathetic little fools
Pretending to be so special
How you feel
How you feel significant

All these things make you strong
You be you
Go on
Be proud of you
Of all the things that shall pass
That shall die
That shall wither away and
Fade away

But

Maybe perhaps
They mean nothing at all
To you
Yet you still
Hold on to anyway
Alas!
Maybe that's all you got

96.

I hate people
I always have
And
I probably always will

They wake up every morning
Shower
Brush their teeth
Have breakfast
Go to work
Come back and have
Dinner
And
Go to sleep
Wake up again the next day
Just to do it the same
All over again

But still they don't care
How can someone be so
Ignorant I think
How can someone be so
Unquestioning

I think
Also
How can someone be so brave
I think

But what are they!
They are a mystery to me
I think they are brave
They prove me
wrong
I think they are chained to routines
They prove me wrong
And I think,
I think for sure,
They are creatures of habit
Hiding under the habitual discomfort
And the challenges of
Their meticulously planned
Unplanned and uncertain schedules
And routines
Every day
Every single day
Alas!
I am wrong
So they intrigue me!

They are beautiful
You! Oh humans!
You are inspiring
You are depressing also

You are caring
But you are very boring too
Yet!
Always so interesting

That's why,
Maybe,
I hate you
Because I cannot admit
How much I love you
How much I envy you
I'm not brave like you
I'm not scheduled like you too
I wish sometimes,
Sometimes only,
I was like you
But unfortunately the sun
And the moon
They cannot be the same

You wait for your turn
Quietly
Silently
And shine like a moon
Whereas I am bound to
Burn like a sun
With all my flaming desires
And blazing imagination
Burning through my skull

And my soul

Someone once said
The sun and the moon
They shine in their own time
Is it my day now?
Or is it your night?
Which is which
Let's leave it for later
For now let me just hate you
Let me secretly envy you
But
I will never let you know
Because I love you

97.

I see you've got some sad little eyes
Giving off smile hiding behind the lies
You're tired and exhausted drowning slowly inside
And with each passing day your soul quietly dies

You want to run away, you want to escape
You just want to burn off like twinkling fireflies

You laugh too hard, yet you try to hold on tight
But I can see all your heart's hidden cries

I see your face and I can surely say
You're full of scars from many a painful sighs

You keep on fighting but it's never enough
It doesn't seem to matter no matter how hard your soul
tries

Your mind has given up, your heart is broken
And your poor body longs to break all the ties

You might smile at the world, but I know all your lies
Because I see that you've got some sad little eyes

98.

Goodbye to all that ever was
All that is now
And all that could have been
With heartfelt condolences

I bow down and pay my respect
To all that passed through
From me
In this time here in this land
Called life

My condolences to all the lonely nights
To all the lost battles
To all the unsuccessful endeavors
Condolences
To all the times my heart got broken
To all the tears shed
In the darkest of times
To all that trying that never made it out
Alive
Those efforts dead and unfruitful

My apologies for all the wrongdoings

I may have participated in
I may have suffered
Or turned a blind eye to
Also to all the desires I couldn't fight hard
Enough for
To those dreams
I wish I could have held on to
More passionately
To those ideas and thoughts
I wish I could have worked on
More vigorously
Apologies
To the life I could never make for myself
For everything I could possibly do
But just couldn't

My gratitude
My eternal gratitude towards life
Towards existence
To everyone and everything I passed by
That touched me
That moved me
That made me who I am
To all the stories I lived
Stories I heard and stories I was included
And invited to
To all the love I have been given
To all the understanding I have been
Bestowed
Gratitude for all the struggles

All the agony
All the ecstasy and the joyful memories
The experiences of the overwhelming realization
Called being alive
Gratitude
To all the opportunities
To all the chances I was given
To all the roads barely taken
I walked through
And the view I was granted for my journey

My condolences
My apologies
And
My eternal gratitude
Towards my life

99.

This is life
Is this life?
An illusion
A stage play
And orchestra
A musical
A drama perhaps
Or a comedy maybe
What is life?
An eternal question it could be
A never-ending search
A prolonged confusion
A satisfactory decision
An idea
A philosophy
A science
An equation

What is life?
A piece of reality?
A slice of experience
Of the cosmos
Of the whole of existence

A smallest fraction of the possibility of
The happenstance itself

My head hurts
Yet
My heart still longs
For the answer
The truth
The definition of life

Is it light?
Or is it darkness?
Is it sorrow
Or just brief joyful occurrences?
What is it?
A profound realization
Or an extremely secret
Veiled mundane notion?
A pact
A tact
A move
A crawl
A flight
A jump
An endeavor
An adventure
A gossip
A conversation between what has been
And what

Longs to be

This life
Is it a voiceless word?
A silent music?
An invisible painting?
A deep, deep well of endless
Desire?
A crossroads of passion
A shower of dead leaves of
Dreams let go
A forked road
A hidden story
A half-burnt cigarette
A half-full whiskey glass
An empty page of a diary
Waiting to be full
Or a scrapbook
Wanting to be completed?

What a question
What a life
The more you ask
The more it eludes you
Making you hold on to
Whatever your identity feels the safest at
Uncomfortably comfortable at perhaps
Inconveniently relaxing at
And the easiest

Most difficult place

Keep on asking
Keep on seeking
The answer is none
The question is one
They say
Think outside the box
Amazing stupidity
Idiocy
Ignorance
Magnificent egoism
Transcendental arrogance
Yet
Sadly
Unfortunately
Our thoughts are inside the box
Our dialogues too
Our existence
Our lives
Our arguments
Our philosophy
Our thoughts
Our ideas
Our seeking
Our longing
Our every piece of hope and despair
Every tears shed
As well as all the times we smiled
All just

Within

Then
What is life?
It is
What it is
Perhaps
Too short to justify
Too long to complain

100.

Reason constrains me
A voice restrains me
I want to burn like a supernova
Explode like a desire
Fly like an impulse
Drive like a lust
Fall like a heart
And
Wander
Wonder
For all of eternity
Like a soul

My body chains me
The world cages me
I want to break free
But
Struggle befriended me a long
Time ago
Before I was born
After I was dead
So long ago
And so far away

I can't remember why
And when
I fell in love with
Chaos

Such sweet mystery
Such illusion
Trapped and enlightening
This feeling of being

One side lies the land of being
Another side calls
The land of self-destruction
And I am stuck in between
The land of possibilities
The land of flux

I am paranoid
I am weird
I am stranger to the ways of both
Worlds
Your words your rhymes
They play in my backyard
Like a dog and a cat
A mere musing
Just words
Simply common ideas

My eyes are dead
My lips so long gone

My hands too lost
And my feet feel
Far too numb

Yet the journey awaits
Yet another adventure
Another story
One more prose
And one more glass of
That sweet bourbon
And
That calming scarring tufts of smoke
Escaping like passing breaths
From the cigarette held
Between my fingers

Something inside me is in turmoil
Still
Something is unsettled
Feels out of place
Out of order
Or lost and not yet found
Or
A habitual comfort of routined discomfort

I feel like a supernova
Held inside a glass bottle
With immense care
And creative engineering
In the eternal deep ocean

Of the cosmos
Just waiting to come ashore
Amidst all the fireworks
In the sky

101.

There's so much that I've written
And so much more I shall ever do
But the best piece of poetry
I shall ever have
Are the ones I hide inside me
Away from the world
Away from everyone

I'd rather have them buried deep
Inside the graveyards of my soul
Than display them like the splendor
Of worldly monuments
For they belong to me
And me only

Maybe I am selfish
Maybe too proud even
But if being called these is the price
I have to pay
Then so be it
For there is so much of what I've written
That I love
They came through me

From the land where
Words and emotions have no bounds
And amalgamate into one
And nothing
And so much I shall ever write
Which will never be known

For I know
There are some things we don't share
Not to everyone
And so are all those words to me
That I shall forever keep hidden

102.

Last night as I was whispering, "No more!"
I heard the Devil knock on my door
He said, "You've given up, I'll take your soul"
I told him it's not over, I'm just very bored

Why do you keep fighting? It is futile
You've run out of tears, run out of smiles
As he told me this I kept on thinking
Stared straight into his eyes without blinking

And told him that although life is very hard
We all have to patiently but play our part
Yes I'm broken, yes I am now hurt
But there's so much fight left in my heart

He seemed amused, looked taken aback even
I told him then there's so much to believe in
Life is our own making and we are the master
Even though time keeps chasing us ever so faster

I am only tired but I haven't given up yet
Because I want to give it all and have no regret
As I told him to leave and wait some more

The Devil smirked quietly and returned back from my door

103.

The closed petal lips
Of budding rose
Longing to kiss the sun
And the rain
Slowly turning ever so red
With each passing moment
Like a soft hidden blush
Which shall melt into a beautiful smile
A bud blossoming into a rose
Like a young maiden
Becoming a woman

Aha!
The bud metamorphoses into
The rose

The rose remembers the journey
Of changing
Of the youth
Feeling the tender warmth of the
Fireball in the sky we
Call sun
And the whispering breeze

Swiftly caressing its petals
The thorns emerging as
Hard sinews of vigilance
Drenched in morning dew

Lost in melancholy
But the rose can hear someone,
Someone is coming
Footsteps getting closer
The gardener is here to water the plants
 Like he always does at this hour

104.

When I was born
I was empty
Just a void
A vessel perhaps for the world to fill
A well perhaps waiting for the rain

And I slowly grew
I grew up
Drenched in the monsoon of experiences
Wet and overflowed with the showers of
The event called life
Ideas, philosophies and thoughts
Languages, aspirations and dreams
Motivations, hopes and longings
Of the systems called society

Then something became "me"
I don't have regrets
Have no remorse
Never have hoped for anything to change
Or alter
And as far as I can tell
Never shall

Because it was just a growing
Just a part of something
Whatever the hell that means

Slowly I "thought"
I became something more
Perhaps just another illusion
Perhaps just another "idea"
Who knows?
I sure as hell don't!

I became nature
I became "me"
An extension too big
Too huge
I thought to myself
Hahahaha
Too transcendental
All just illusion
Or just a part of growing?
An ebb and flow
Perhaps an escape
Don't ask me from what?
Or where though
'Cause I honestly do not know

Every stepping stone seems like mirage to me
Now
I feel everything is just passing by
And I stand at the same spot

Watching the sunset
And the sunrise
The cool breeze blowing from the ocean
The moon shining down on me
Like I was something special
What a load of bullshit!
And the flowers turning to me
Just to admire the tumultuous
Yet beautiful hardship-filled
Inspirational journey
The world calls life
Well, who knows?
I am just comparing!
I don't know shit

But what am I?
What am I becoming?
When does it stop?
Or better yet
When did it fucking start?
I want to know
I really really do
But alas!
All in vain
I like to believe
This is an eternally futile poking
Hahahaha

Spices of love and emotions
Boiled on the tempestuous stove of existence

Everyone is trying to escape
At least that's what I believe
Nothing to be alarmed of though
Just a routine existential phenomenon
Some same
Some a little different in chronological order
But what the hell
Still the same

I don't know what I was
When I was born
I shall never know what I am
Or
When I will cease to exist
I dare use the word "death"
I was just being romantic
With life

Fun
Enjoyment
Struggles
Challenges
Hopes
Dreams
Aspirations
Inspirations
Fame
Success
Love
Life

It is what is!
It truly is
But if you think about it
It hurts your head

Maybe you shouldn't think
But
Just live it
The way it comes
Like the ebb and flow of the ocean
Simply natural
Letting it be

Ah!
But a distressed soul
Can ever so only hope for the peace
Of a routine
Or is it too cruel to ask for it?
Or too wrong?
I don't know
I really don't know!

105.

Some faces we wear as masks
Some masks we wear as faces
Hiding some deep dark secrets
Buried within without any traces

There's a mask for every occasion
And a face for every mask
It keeps switching back and forth
Depending on time and place and task

Some do it ever so willingly
Some do it without their own consent
Some acknowledge the need for masks
Some love the deliberate concealment

They blend together after some time
And some forget which is which
Some get lost in this whole process
And they can never again switch

Everyone does it all the time
Some realize it and some are unaware
The faces and masks go on and on

Kailash Darji

No one can stop it, no one will dare

Some faces fall in love with masks
Some masks fall in love with faces
In a world full of variety of characters
Maybe our real face never leaves any traces

106.

I walk into a shop
Just an ordinary one

The lady welcomes me with a
Big smile
With her thinly trimmed arched high
Eyebrows
And sharpened cheekbones
With her heavy makeup trying to hide the
Unhappy wrinkles life gave her
From changing jobs
Working in places like this

Moving from one shop to another
Greeting random, boring
Customers like me
Watching strange pedestrians
Walking down the streets
And roads
Getting into shops
To buy things they don't want
With the money they don't have

To live the life they don't like

As I am looking around to see
If there's anything I want
She asks, "May I help you with anything, sir?"
With her botoxed lips
What do I tell her?
I just went in to see her up close

I say, "Sorry, must be the wrong shop"
She smiles again
And tells me
To come back again
If I need anything
And that
She would love to help me
Get what I want

107.

This forest is made of buildings
This city is full of lost souls
Lonesome streets
Lost, empty walls
And
So many lives facing death
All by themselves
So many more living their lives
Alone

A concrete jungle of bricks and sticks
Cold and damp
Wet and slippery
Hot and bright
Whatever the seasons bring
Ever alive
Ever growing
The skyscrapers of this forest
Longing to touch the sky
Leaning to kiss the stars
Forever on the go
Like a beating heart

Undead before it's dead

People on street
They look like they are lost
Funny thing is
They know where they are going
But the wind blows cold
And the yellow leaves fall down
The brown leaves get blown away
And the green leaves are plucked from their branches
Way too early
And people hold themselves tight
Wrap themselves warm
But keep on walking anyway

Looking at this city
No one can say it's not a forest
Bushes of small houses
Streams of trains and buses
Ever-flowing river of cars
And fishlike people
Swimming
Always swimming away around the
Mountains of supermarkets
Huge fields of shops and restaurants
All enveloped under the
Canopy of bright lights
And giant skyscrapers

How easy it is to

Get lost here
And just like a maze
How hard it is to
Leave

108.

You talk and talk and talk
But you never speak
Forever you stay hidden
Without letting anyone take a peek
You keep your head open
Yet you keep your heart guarded
You never let anyone get close
Ending all before it even started

Your lips long to say so much
'Cause there's so much inside your head
Yet you choose to stay silent
And you act ignorant instead
You feel like a lost wanderer
Lost alone in the journey of life
Ever so aware of the world around
Full of harmony yet full of strife

You try to learn as much as you can
You take it all in but you can't let go
And I think it gets overwhelming sometimes
You know it has taken its toll
You see the patterns repeated

In circles the world goes round and round
People and places with stories of ages
Forever lost and never found

And you feel everything and see it all
It's a shame you can't do anything
Words and voices and stories and pictures
Sheltered in your head are so many things
Yet you try to make something out of it
Hard although it may be but you do try
Your head is a mess and your heart's hurt
Still you don't speak, you just silently deny

109.

When the heaven cries and sheds tears of rain
Making it fall on earth washing away all the pain
Everything seems rejuvenated with beauty reawakened
Nature starts blushing just like a fair maiden

The rivers and rivulets with their waves start dancing
The clear tufts of white clouds can be seen advancing
It feels so fresh, the world seems so clean
The mountains and the sky look as if they're romancing

The green becomes greener, the trees dripping wet
The sky comes out of dark clouds' silhouette
The air smells of renewal, the earth feels relaxed
Rain comes and washes away all of yesterday's regret

Happiness is abundant, it feels joyous again
Puddles of water in the streets and in the lane
Bringing together alike all the old, the young and the
children
Everything becomes beautiful when the rain embraces
in its domain

110.

Sometimes
I look at my wall
And I feel like punching
And then sometimes
I punch it
Like really hard
Sometimes many times too
The wall doesn't care
I hurt my knuckles a little
But hey!
Who cares?
I don't
They get a little bruised
But I'll live

Sometimes
I look in the mirror
And I feel like punching it to pieces
Shattering it
Breaking apart all the lies it tells me
All the hypocrisy it holds
But I don't!
I simply can't

For I know
I have to wake up every morning
And look in that mirror

Also
I already got a wall
To punch
And it won't break
At least it hasn't
That is until now

111.

Society is a cruel thing
Yet utterly necessary too
A necessary evil you can say!

It has its ups and downs
Perhaps
More downs than ups
But that's just us
Hey!
We are only the members who are complaining
But this is democracy
Right?
Majority wins

The individual suffers
Complains
Bitches
Struggles
But we know
When we all individuals get together
We suffer from hypocrisy
We are scared
To speak our mind

To be individuals again
But
Only in the midst of a crowd
Or a "public" like they say
Pity us!

The systems were developed
Lifestyles were preordained
Roles were assigned
But we should know better
The job has to be done
If we don't do it
Who will?
If we don't do it today
When then?

But is it worth the individual's sacrifice?
Living for the greater good
Or so they say

The wheel has to keep on
Turning
The cycle must never be
Broken
That's society
No matter how civilized
It claims itself to be
How advanced
It hopes itself to be
How happy

It imagines itself to be
That is far from the truth

We are not unhappy
We are just not at peace!

But society is not peace
We are mere
Pawns!
We dream of ourselves as king and queen
But alas
Reality is just narcissistic romanticism
Just an illusion

So
This is what we got
It is
What it is

We have no choice but to be us
You be you
I'll be me
This is our only freedom
Only solace
Only escape
Only salvation
What a heavy word
"salvation"

Society

Not something we need
But
Definitely
Something we deserve

112.

A young boy walks
The prairies of the world
Finding the way
Looking ahead
Moving forward
Growing up
Growing up

Traveling through the valleys of youth
Bruised palms
Steady feet
He meets every adventure with dignity
With grace
Humble yet unwavering
Strong and unyielding
He keeps walking on
Through the forests
And rivers and streams
Rocky terrain
Unwinding trails
Forever lost pathways
Nobody dares to take

Making his own way

The boy continues his journey
Ever going on
Until his eyes kiss all the stars
Until he has breathed in
The north wind down his lungs
Embraced the sun in his shadows
And
Held the moon in his arms
Every night

The time passes by
Slowly but surely
One day at a time
One moment at a time
The boy keeps growing

His journey leads him to a
Mountain
That he has to climb
Mountain of experience
A mountain to test
The lessons he has
Learned
In all his journey
The whispers of morning mist
The seductions of dusky horizon
The playfulness of the flowers and

Fireflies
The coyness of blushing autumn leaves
Fluttering like butterflies
In the still lake of
His voyage
He reminisces them all
Cherishing their adversities
Their beauty

He climbs uphill
He claims the way
He moves upwards
Up and up he goes
Through snaky paths
Through bushes and canopies of
Shades
Midst the skyscrapers of tall oak trees
And pine
And sophisticated fir trees
His feet get tired but they don't
Stop
They keep climbing
For this is his test
This is his journey
Ending
Finally

He passes through the clearing of his conscience
And comes to an opening
A space to breathe

A place to rest
He stops his feet
For the first time to
Take in the world
Absorb the view
Of his destination
Watching over the long and
Winding roads he took
To reach here

The misty mountain glistens in the
Sun
The enveloping fog moves through the forests
And valleys
And rivers
Like a smooth silk shawl
The prairies far gone
And disappeared somewhere
Beyond the horizon
Somewhere really far away

The boy realizes that he is
No longer
The same as when he first left
On his travel
For now he has come home
He lets out a long sigh
Now
He understands
For now

He is no longer a boy
For now
He is a
Man

113.

Some lost
Some forgotten
Some still wandering about
In the realm between
A dream and imagination

Some loved
Some left alone
Some untouched
And some frequently visited

Some bringing tears of joy
Some causing a lump
In the chest
Looking back now
Some seem so distant
Some still feel so fresh
Like it happened
Just yesterday

Some feel like lessons
Some feel like a loss
Some a blessing

And some feel like a curse
Hardships and tragedies
Achievements and longings
Playful banters some
And some
Hurtful agonies

But all of them still
Stuck inside a tiny brain
Yet held together
By unknown threads
Weaved into the eternal tapestry
Of heart

These memories
Maybe
They are our only possessions
The only thing we can truly
Claim to be ours
In this life cradled by
Death
Some sweet
And some painful
Yet
Just ours
Only
Ours

114.

Sins
Your greatest temptations!
The ones that are forbidden
The ones claimed a curse
The sins
They tell a lot about a man
Than all his apparent sainthood

The lust in his eyes when he
Looks at love
The envy he feels the way
He lacks
The slothful nature of his
That sometimes just gives up
And his pride
That prevents him from achieving the victory
In surrender of the self
This greed in him
To know so evermore
And live so evermore

Those eyes of his
They want to consume everything

Those hands long to feel
Everything
That heart of his
It desires to hold
All of time and space
And everything beyond
And the soul
The soul keeps accumulating all
Always
Forever
Till eternity
Forever taking in

And the anger
He feels towards his sins
Towards himself

The devil is a man
And the man is just a saint
Repenting too much
Or maybe
Just not enough

115.

Lest we forget
Says these pathetic fools

The war memorial down the road
From my house
Is empty all
Through the year
No respects
No visitors
Maybe few
Just the loved ones of the
Brave ones that died
Fighting for the ungrateful bunch
Of morons
The fools that died

All through the year
No heads bow down
No flowers turn up
Just some tourists taking pictures
And making up stories
Some vagabonds drinking
Teens unappreciative of the sacrifice

So-called "adults"
Ignorant of their valiance
Of those who fought
And couldn't come back home to
Their loved ones

All through the year
I walk by
Look at the names
Try to imagine their lives
Their courage
Their fight
But no one seems to care
No one gives a damn

But once every year
The war memorial becomes a shrine
A temple of resolution and
Gallantry
An abode of "respect"
The flowers pour in
The candles are lit
Wishes and prayers are offered
And then
No more
Just silence
Same old ignorance
Until the statue rusts
Until the mold slowly takes over
Inch by inch

Day by day

And no one comes
No one cares
Just a memorabilia
Just a lump of lifeless
Metal
The war memorial stays like this
Until that one day
That one day of the year
When it shall be
Revered again

Lest we forget
What a joke!

116.

Yes
These eyes were the same dark brown
Before I met you too
Looking at the world
In all its glory
I thought nothing special of them
Just the usual
My hair too
I felt was all right
It was a little brunette
But I would make do with it
And the nose and the lips
They were fairly good enough
To get me by
Pass me off as a normal
Human specimen

I thought
I was just normal
Nothing special
Just ordinary
Then I met you

And I saw how much you loved me
You shook me to my core
My beliefs
My ideas
My opinions about myself
And the world
You made me see the beauty
Of the world
Like I was baptized
And born anew
A new life
A new set of eyes that saw differently
A new
Me

How you made me feel
Special
Feel extraordinary
How you loved me so much
Accepted me for
Who I was
And made me fall in love with you
But more importantly
You made me fall in love with
Myself again

I guess that's what
Beautiful people do
In love

117.

When I die
Leave me alone

Don't burden me with the
Stories of our memories
Don't endow me with false praises
And untrue glory
Leave me be

When I die
Leave my body alone
Don't touch it
You don't have to clean it
For god's sake
Don't change my clothes too
God
Even in death you want to exercise your
Control over me?
Your normality?
Your values?
Just leave me be

My family

My brotherhood
My humanity
Just let me die

Oh yeah
Just one other thing
Burn me down on a pyre
So my soul can escape into the wind
And kiss the rustling leaves
And love the dainty daffodils
On the mountains
And my ashes
They are the remnants of my vessel
My body
Pour them in the river
I shall meet with my love Ocean at last
And shall forever dream
In her deep sleep

118.

Hello happiness! My old friend
We almost met each other, many a times
I thought the gloomy days'd never end
On my heart laden with sorrow's crimes

I had almost forgotten your merry face
I long for you to just be with me today
Before the pangs of sorrow shall chase
Me down to the river, where its children stay

Those growing griefs slowly drowning me
And the vines of agony binding me tight
I restlessly wait for the day when I can see
You 'cause I am over this futile fight

I want to smile, laugh, and enjoy the sun
Come and help me drive away the sadness
Oh happiness my comrade, how bright you burn
In my heart I've spared you your favorite place

But alas! We keep missing each other
By chance or other reasons unknown

While this pain quietly creeps up to smother
And this misery seems to just forever grow

My compatriot! You have forsaken my life
And left me in the hands of such dejection
I cannot proceed further with this frightful strife
I try to be brave but the loneliness doesn't lessen

Hello, happiness! My old friend
I keep fighting this war with gloomy days
In the hopes of seeing you someday again
While my rejected and lost spirit herein stays

119.

The deathly quiet of the night
Falls silently on my ears
I can hear the abrupt yet loud
Thunderous crashing of the waves
Far away
And the slow tick of the time
Passing by
Slowly but swiftly

Utterly vacant
And incredibly full
The night brings in treasures of
Dreams and nightmares
The roads have stopped making noise too
After a hard day's work
Resting peacefully
Lights off in all the houses
Only the streetlights are awake
I hear a cat meowing
Anxious crickets chirping
A faint flutter of the night owl
Calmly perched somewhere

Vigilant yet awake perhaps

My own heart beating
Pumping blood to every part of my body
Like everything inside me has a life
Of its own
Making me breathe
Making me feel
Making me "me"

They tell me
It's time
To close my eyes and drift away
For the night is too still tonight
But my heart is still longing
For some unknown adventure
Of tomorrow

120.

Oh, beautiful stars my friend
You burn so bright like
The glow of a supernova
Like thousand exploding suns
Like a lonesome lamp in the
Vacant skies of the space so deep

Just like the thump in my heart
When I hear God
When I hear love
You keep beating from afar
Twinkling
Burning
Always burning
With the same passion that burns in my
Heart too

You and me
We are compatriots in this eternal creation
Sharing the same stardust that created everything
You have a piece of my soul
Just like I possess

A slice of your dazzle

You are living in the past
And the times long gone
But I can see you only from
The eyes of your tomorrow
We are separated by this deep gulf of
Time
Eons and eons between us
Oh, stars!
My heavenly comrades!
How far we are
Yet still so close
And bound to each other
Through the fabric of space

121.

Each morning
I wake up to the drums of
Having to attend to all the worldly
Affairs

I take a shower to wash myself away
Everything that constitutes me
To make me "me"
Taking a deep breath
Like I am deep underwater
And I look in the mirror
All fogged up by the warm steam of the shower
That has cleansed me
That has baptized me of all the
Things that resist to venture out
Into the routine
Of my social endeavors

I draw a happy face in the mirror
With my fingers
Slowly
Practicing my happy face
My smile

And I exercise my normative greetings
And goodbyes
They always come in handy
When I awake in between my
Pretenses
Throughout the day

Tired and exhausted from all the acting
And pretending
I come home at night
Always late
Then I go to the shower
My only refuge
To wash away all the burdens of the day gone by
All the heavy enactments of the hours
That I have played part in
To clean, scrub, scour
And
Wipe down all the traces of
Someone I was not
All day long

Just to wake up next morning
After a sleepless night of
Nightmares from all my theatrics
Performed yesterday
Just to wash myself in the shower again
Hide myself again

And I draw a happy face

In the same foggy mirror
To practice my smile again

122.

What makes us isn't there
At all
All the constituents that make everything
The particles and forms we believe in
They don't exist
Well, maybe they do
But you can only perceive their
Existence
In vague forms of vibration
And energy signatures
Not yet visible to our
Naked eyes

The empty spaces of
Atoms and also
What makes them
End up creating shapes
And filling up spaces
Somehow
Creating the material existence
We call world
And the universe
And the reality

And all that there is

So we see things
That really aren't there
But they are too
Unobserved although
They still exist and are

The illusion of possibilities
That are the building blocks
Of the skyscrapers of the physical world
This dimension
Are baffling in themselves
A paradox
A mystery
A magic
Of the cosmic strands
Utterly necessary yet
Incredibly enigmatic
And hidden from the plain view

123.

He is a lone wolf
Marking his own way
Through the dark forest
Leaving his footprints in the
Cold white snow

He hunts
He runs
He makes his own life
A battle for survival
All he's ever learned
All he's ever done

Unafraid
Unconcerned of all
And unknown
The lone wolf keeps going on
Passing through new territories
Building his strength
Testing himself

Resilient and adamant
Throbbing with willpower vast

He is
The lion may be the king
He may claim the jungle
But the lone wolf
Walks on the sunlight
Bathes in the canopy of Milky Way
And
He kisses the moon
Every night
And that is the prize
Only he can claim

124.

This is a land of lies
This is a land of ties
Of all worldly affairs
Of smiles and cries

Fashioned with blood and bone
Yet stranded alone
The world keeps on turning
With an eternal silent moan

Earth, water, fire and air
Hatred, love, God and fear
Fantasies, dreams and imaginations
Come, find everything here

Born in the cradle of death
Mere whisper of creation's breath
Mysterious is life's existence
Devoid of hope yet full of faith

Stars burn vehemently in the sky
Life passes down here quietly by

This land too will cease to be
One day but unfortunately without a goodbye

125.

The crisis looms over our head
The problem persists
They say,
"Little knowledge is dangerous"
But to whom?
To the one who possesses
That knowledge?
Or to the one
It is used for?
Or
To the one it is used
Against?
And how much is little?
What is knowledge anyway?
The sword is still hanging by our
Necks

Knowledge is a double-edged sword
Tempting
Yet laden with hefty penalty too
Cuts through the blade of grass
And the tufts of clouds
Just as easily

Pierces the dark veil of ignorance
But can stab the sun itself too
Killing the light
The dilemma still exists

And action is something different
Altogether
A shadow of the knowledge
Reflected by expression
Judgmental
Biased
Impure
Mistaken
Striving
Physical
Necessary
Utterly necessary piece
Of the puzzle called reality
Or creation
Or life
As we might call it!

The crisis never dies
Has been since time immemorial
Forever shall be
Acknowledgment of knowledge
Is the root of all worldly affairs
Of all worldly problems
Sometimes I believe,

At least I like to think I do,
"Ignorance is bliss"

126.

Life
It is an arrow
When let go from the
Grip of the bow called birth
It flies through the adventure of
Its own
It flies
And it flies
Moving through time
Through air
Through the cosmos
Slowly
Softly
Steadily
To hit the bull's-eye

What if it hits the bull's-eye?
What if it doesn't?
Is the target predetermined?
Or is it where the arrow falls?
The target is the death
It is the bull's-eye
It is the final resting place

Everything else
Is just life

127.

Look at these graveyards of empty roads
Going nowhere
But reaching everywhere
All on their own
Without any passengers
Without any destination
Yet never ending

Like an abandoned graveyard
The roads are empty
No flowers on this spot
No wishes wished here
No visitors on this part of the
Cemetery
Forgotten graveyard of roads
That once was full of
Awake and traveling lives

128.

Silent
Pensive
Hidden away from the world
In a quiet corner
Knitting his own webs of thoughts
And his life
Goes on
Elated in his solitude
And gifted with the knowledge
Of being
He lives stealthily
Like stifled steps
Tiptoeing in the quiet of the night
How he gets in and
Out of the world

He lives in a house alone
All in his remoteness
His routines in seclusion
All the while
His thoughts keep knitting
His paths all taken
Making a web

He looks around his room
And he sees a spider
Up on the wall in a
Corner
On its web
With its sticky legs
Silent
Pensive
Hidden away from the world

129.

With the veil of mist and mask of snow
To flaunt her beauty, winter says hello
The cold days come, chilly nights linger
And the cruel Northern wind never stops to blow

Winter clads all of nature in color white
Makes everyone seek shelter, and hide
The withered plants stay covered in winter snow
And a strong smell of iciness hovers at night

The hills, the trees, the nature hides away
With a longing of warm summer's sunny day
People gather and share stories around the fireplace
Fowls and beasts in their nests and dens stay

Nature's window has now freezing white drapes
Frostbiting carpets of grass and all landscapes
And people wait patiently with the whole of nature
For winter to end but enjoying every falling snowflakes

130.

Some days
It's all right
I go about my day
Follow my scheduled routines
Have a coffee at my favorite cafe
Do my work chores
Perform my duties
Engage with the world
Put on a brave face
Fight the battle till the last bell rings
And I leave the ring
To come back home
And wash myself
Of the day

Other days
I am at peace
When I don't have to enter the ring

131.

Don't you despair, don't you worry
Live for today and don't be sorry
The world will stop, the world will turn
To wait and see how brightly you burn

Don't give up friend, you must try
And make it all worthwhile before you die
Your mind is the sky, your heart is the sea
You were forever meant to be free

If you fall, give yourself a hand
Be brave my friend and understand
Though you suffer defeats or get scars
Your story will be etched in the stars

To live life with memories and lessons
Fight your battles with strongest passions
Because I hope you know what you're capable of
You can rule all the worlds, both below and above

132.

We all live
We all love
We thrive and fight
We fail, we succeed
Some battles we win
Sometimes we retreat
We embrace our failures
Celebrate the victories
Experience life's adversities
And any joyous moments we can gather

We all put in efforts
We all try
We all make believe
We smile, sometimes we cry
From dawn till dusk
We have a role to play
Before we slowly creep into
The warm embrace of dreams
Closing our eyes
Tired and exhausted
Done for the day

We are all born
We shall someday surely
Die
And leave behind moments
In our loved ones' hearts
A fragment of remembrance
A trace of our life's footprints
In the sands of time
A piece of our soul
Before we disintegrate
And blow into the wind
Flow into the river
Our ashes will rust and be collected
As a mountain
Our bones will decay
And fall in the deep abyss of the ocean
To be pearls again
Perhaps
It is true
Perhaps
It isn't

But hope we must
Have faith we must
We have to keep going
We have to believe
For I think all we ever try
In this brief life
A fleeting breath
Just a stopgap

Is to say
Is to announce to the world
To the cosmos
That
We existed
We lived
We loved
We lived as humans
Stretching out our hands to the moon and stars
Burning and blazing just like the sun
Just passing by for all we know
But
That we were here
We were

133.

Ah
I don't have to drink again
I quit
'Cause there's nothing to gain
No more to lose
No loneliness to avoid
No void to fill
No emotions to escape
No world to run from
And no hurt
To hide away from

No
I don't have to smoke again
Nowhere to fly away to
No place to run off to
No thoughts to stop coming
Nothing to let me touch
And injure me

No, I don't have to do that again
I'm done
They were promising

Oh yes they were
But I always knew
Always
They were just full of false promises
Never with the courage to fulfill
What they said they'd do
Promised me a beautiful death
Instead
Just poisoned my days

134.

You say
You live to be alive
To feel alive
You live for life
You say
Untrue
False words
You live for your death
Every moment of your life has been
To give justification
To your death
An explanation
A reasoning
A conversation
And
A persuasion

You live to succeed in death
Death is all you
Ever
Cared for
That is all you've ever lived for

Your false promises
And all your fake
Hopes and dreams
Aspirations and false words
Oh!
These words you claim
You live for life
Such a shame!
You have and
Will always
Forever
Exist for your death
Breathe
Waiting for the time it
Stops

For some flowers on your deathbed
And some fond memories
Perhaps
That will make you immortal
With the ones who
Live to tolerate you

135.

Once I was sitting on a
Park bench
Minding my own business
Then came a woman
Good looking I should add
And she sat on my lap

I wasn't feeling social that particular day
Not that I ever am!
But who cares, right?
So she sat in my lap
And started giving me a
Cheap imitation of a
Lap dance

Me?
I wasn't amused at all
I politely asked her to
Get off
To no avail
I asked her again
No response
I requested her furthermore
To leave me alone

And not invade my personal
Privacy
Which at that point had turned into
A sexual one
She wouldn't however budge
A single inch

So frustrated
I grabbed her boobs
And started fondling them
Startled she jumped off
And started screaming insults at me
Called her cameraman mate
Hidden nearby
In plain view

Crowd gathered
Situation worsened
Upholders of the law arrived
I was taken into custody

Needless to say
I had to spend a night
In jail
But I told myself
Consoled myself
The scales of justice is
Always skewed
The balance is never
Balanced

136.

Every thought is a piece of land
Its accepted validity a territory
Its empirical proof
Its legality

As many heads
As many nationalities
All its maneuvers to trace
And map the cosmos
Just educated assumption
A leap of faith
I call it
A breath of common sense

Trapped inside a blue bottle
Of imagination
Surrounded by an infinite
Void of ignorance
They keep probing
They keep poking the
Reality

137.

When I was a kid
I used to sometimes burn the sugar
To give color to my tea
Because I couldn't find the jar
We kept our tea leaves in
My mother used to say
That's not a tea
It's just sweet hot water

I used to say then
It has the color
And the taste
It is tea

The world always has masters
The gurus
The so-called enlightened ones
Who serve sweet elixir of
Their knowledge
To the poor common folk

But nobody asks them
Where are the tea leaves?

138.

When I get too drunk
My vision multiplies
Last night
As usual
I was too far gone
I went to get a glass of water
Got confused
Which glass to pick

The spiritual masters
Are intoxicated too in their own
Little world of spirituality
And their "consciousness"

That's why
Maybe
They call this world
An illusion

139.

Good friends are like fine wine
You talk and talk
But get intoxicated slowly
Quietly
And the next day
You're fine

Bad friends on the other hand
They hit you hard
And give you a migraine
For days

140.

Nothing is as patient as trees
They wait and wait
And wait
Yet
Keep growing just the same
Longing to touch the stars
Hold the moon in its embrace
And kiss the sky

Nothing is as desperate as an animal
Always acting on an impulse
Reacting just for survival
And propagation

Then
There's us
Maybe that's why
We devour them both
And
Destroy ourselves in the process

141.

Once I was walking
And people started screaming at me
"Madman! Madman!"
They threw stones at me
Attacked me
Verbally and physically
Very much so

So
I started running
They chanted
"Look! The madman is running away"
If I were a madman, I wouldn't run
I ran precisely because
I wasn't one

142.

Once
A spiritual master was preaching
On a hilltop
To a crowd of devotees
And common folk about human attachments
And all the mortal ailments
We suffer thus

So I stole his begging bowl
And ran away
Then he furiously started
Chasing me downhill
With his staff

143.

Let me tell you a story
Of how I fell in love
With a prostitute

When I went to her
She welcomed me with open arms
No admonishments for how I was
No judgments for who I was
Only acceptance
Of course her hospitality
Wasn't free of charge!
I had to trade something too
But then again
What is?

As she stripped off what little
She had on
I was getting a glimpse of the
Divine
As one by one
Slowly her garments fell down
So did my religious beliefs
Ideologies and philosophies

And she rode me on her
Golden chariot
Around the seven heavens
The cosmos
And all the while
Letting me ask questions
God sure was generous!

When I was tired of the
Cosmic tour
And reached my climax
She stroked my hair
Well!
That wasn't the only thing
And she was smiling
Petting me like a curiously
Tired child
And she asked me
How do you feel?

She asked me if I wanted
Another go at the
Roller coaster
I said
Let me catch my breath first
This has been very spiritual
Let me take it slowly
Yet she was patient
God sure works in mysterious ways

And waited she patiently
Until we went off again

When I left
I gave her some extra offerings
Saying this has been very educational

And when I was walking out
I thought to myself
Heaven and hell really are real
They are both right here

144.

What tiny lives you live
What pathetic lives you lead
What puny desires you chase
What small thoughts you bear

What hypocrite life you build
You long for death and
What lies beyond
As an insurance
For the accident that is your life
For the disaster that you've made of
this existence

You live your life as something
As trivial as a chance
As an opportunity for a repair
Or betterment
Or perhaps in the hopes of an
Upgrade
For what comes next

Fool
It is what it is

Learn this
You are the universe
In a flux
Caught between the time and space
And consciousness
This one life is all you get

Break the cages of your
Thoughts and your excuses
Fly little bird
Fly into the limitless sky!

145.

He is one battle you can't
Win by fighting
Surrender yourself
Fall at his feet
Ask for forgiveness
Absolve yourself
And all your arrogance

He is one knowledge
You will never reach
Unless you abandon your logic
Your faith, your belief
Your words and your thoughts
Abandon yourself
And the world

If you want to let go
And reach him
Accept everything there is
The good, the bad,
The ugly, everything
And you'll see
He was always with you

It was you
Who was always running away
From him
All your life

146.

Still
Reeling from the aftershock of
Having been baptized as human
Walking down the crowded
Desolate streets
Looking at these historic long-dead
Pavements and walls
Smelling coffee beans and
Cheese and ham croissants
I feel lost

The ocean grunts like an old woman
Who's left ignored in a corner
Of a family gathering to amuse herself
To entertain herself
Her waves though
Violently lapping
Furiously crashing on the shore
Like a child's tantrum
Unheeded by people
Uncared by pedestrians
Too lost in the smell of
Morning coffee

Their morning poison
Their choice of toxin
A happy drug

And then
I look at these caffeinated faces
And cheesy smiles
Fully tested and ready to rush
About
They look like they had
A good night's sleep
And woke up too early with
Sunrise
And here I am
Feeling like crap!

147.

The moonlight dances with the
shadows in my room
Slowly chasing any traces of
Twilight away
The sun is sinking under the ocean waves
Hiring with the moon's entrance
Upon the stage of night

The gold dies down and
The silver drapes over the world
Like a lost memory, moon shines
And like my lover
She smiles at me
winks at me

And I keep vigil at the window
With the dancing shadows of my room
Staring at the cool sea breeze
Fitting with the trees
And their branches and
Leaves
Drenched in the silvery white paint
Of the moonlight

Oh, moon!
How you chased away my dreams too!
How you made my sleep
Hide away tonight

148.

Tirelessly
Continuously
With each passing moment
With every fleeting second
Minutest of the minutes
In the hour hand of the clock
Along with the traveling sun
Westward from the east
At the onset of every dawn
The day goes on

One day after another
Repeating itself
Aging every day yet full of newness
Full of amelioration
Filled with novelty
Bringing adventures untold from the
Uncertain embrace of the tomorrow
Unborn yet
And memories and experiences
From the deepest depths of the
Past almost forgotten
The day goes on

Bringing gifts of joy
And sometimes a Pandora's box of
Agony and griefs
But the day has no control over them all
Cannot escape them all
All it keeps doing is
Guiding you by your hopeful fingers
Holding you by your faith
Lighting that fire of expectations in your soul
And burning the fuel of your
Imagination
Through the darkest of nights
Into the wonderful land of what shall come to be
Just for you
Handmade by fate only to your design
The day goes on
The day goes on

And all it also for is
All it begs you to do is
Have a little faith
And just believe
In the day
One day at a time

149.

Words, smiles and gestures
They seem so trivial
Yet they are so very important

Wise words can lift people up
Words in anger
Can hurt deeper than a paper cut
Perhaps even deeper sometimes
Into someone's soul too

And smiles
When strangers see you smile
At them
While passing by
Walking by
Or traveling somewhere
Immediately brings smile to their faces too
Helps keep that light go on
Maybe just a little
But still worth it

When you gesture someone out of goodwill
They love it

Everyone is fighting their battles
Their war raging inside
And outside their world
A simple act of love
Of care
Of kindness does go a long way
And likewise your rudeness
And your disregard towards them
Pains them slightly
Or if their hearts are sensitive
Can wound them

Just remember next time
When a stranger smiles at you
On the street
A total stranger
Yet they share their wounded little spark of sunshine
Their smile at you
And tell you to have a good day
Know that
Words, smiles and gestures
They can change the world
One person at a time

150.

I am staring at the night
A black black night
No stars around
The moon long dead
The trees stand high
Laughing at mankind
You killed everything
You killed us all
At least this void of a view is all you got
At least

The fireflies burn close by
Flying around whispering embers of despair
Lightening the light of death
And all that ends in the end
The buildings a ruin
The roads all empty
The life is all but gone
Nothing but the dust

Everything pointing fingers at me
I am the last one
The only one left to blame

Can't blame them
The survivor of the apex predator
Last of the species
Remnants of the violence that kissed the existence
To destruction
To the end
To the ultimate collapse

But there's a faint sound
A whistling of the wind
A thump of the waves crashing
But just a memory
Like a desolate heartbeat
An echo of the silence
Slowly dissipating into the darkness
All that's left

Why am I the only one?
How come?
What happened?
Nevertheless
The end is nigh
The night is high
Death embraces us all
All that is me of course
There is peace
An eternal kind we
I mean humankind looked for all their life
Those hypocrites!
Oh yeah

I must be one of them by now

I can hear the reverberations of the memories of cars
passing by my streets
People talking of their nonsensical
Meaningful everyday endeavors
Stories of their lives
Their loved ones
Their enmities
Their accomplishments
Their gossips
And all sorts of other things

I see the lights
Just a mirage though
A remembrance of the lights that used to be lit
At homes they called then
I did too, no more but now
Nothing but sands now
Nothing but dust now

All that's left is guilt
A kind that is bestowed very much responsibly
Very much morally
Whatever that means now
All the meaning is lost now
With all the minds that held the meaning of
Its constitution
And I am not a judge
Not an advocate

But still a culprit
Still the lawbreaker
Or at least one of them
Prosecution is nigh
I am to be hanged
With eternal solitude
With everlasting loneliness
With a sentence of forever being by myself
Till everything ceases to be
Ceases to exist
In a desolate
Foreign land of nothingness
Left with all my musings
With my thoughts
My blank imaginations that fill through the
Past and all the futures
That shall never be
And all that's dead which no longer
Have any meaning
What is meaning?

The night is dark
The fireflies are the last ones to go
Other than me
I know I am a criminal
I know
I am a part of the existential accountability
But still
Let me enjoy this
Let me enjoy my despair

Let me enthrall in this unknown
Be amazed by this cessation
Be taken aback by this unexpected turn of
Highly anticipated turn of events
Let me be "me" till death
Full of my private corruptions
My personal reconciliations
My identities
The constituents of me being "me"

Let the world end
Let it all end
I know I have no control
I grieve
But just
Let me be me
For a while